Best Little
TEEN GUIDE EVER

Power House

Best Little
TEEN GUIDE
EVER

40 Success Principles for a Rewarding Life Experience

PAMELA PEREZ
The Education Therapist™

"Best Little Teen Guide Ever!"

POWER HOUSE
AN IMPRINT OF POWER HOUSE STUDIOS LLC

thepowerhousestudio.com

SECOND EDITION

Specialty Graphics Design by Sarah Fernandez for POWER HOUSE

Power House Studios, LLC.
PO Box 101678 Cape Coral FL 33910
Home of the Power House Blueprint™ - The 90-Days Vision into Sight Concierge Publishing System
ISBN# 978-1-7321423-0-5 (eBook) ISBN# 978-1-7321423-1-2 (Paperback Book)

INTRODUCTION

This teen guidebook is one of a kind! Its principles deliver a basic foundation of psychological and social concepts and ideas that have existed for ages. If you have a teenager or work with teens, this is a great little investment for their future. These principles are not taught in school, they are taught in life.

This small guidebook simply lists 40 various life principles, a coordinating quote, and a reflection question attached to each principle. For example, Principle #2 is entitled "Increase Your Level of Emotional Intelligence." This describes a process beginning with thoughts, which lead to emotions, which finally lead to behavior. The lesson here is to help young people become aware of their own behavior and the sources from where it originates. Principle #11 is entitled "Watch Who You Hang Around" and describes the principle of influence with regard to a person's five closest relationships. Principle #29 is entitled "Forgive Often and Don't Hold Grudges," which explains the power of release versus the bondage of offense and anger.

Hopefully, this helps to paint a picture of this little guidebook for teens. It is a short read as each principle is on one page with a corresponding quote and reflection question, followed by a journal page with reflection prompts and a "doodles and dreams" page. This teen guide is designed as a 40 day experience which can be easily taught within a family devotion, youth group, or academic setting. The principles are written with big and bold letters so as to be easily viewed as one flips through the guidebook.

My experience as a 15 year veteran high school teacher has taught me that most teens would rather look at pictures and big words than read large amounts of fine print. My hope is that every teen who will study and apply these 40 principles will embark on a journey of self discovery, a life journey that holds meaning and purpose.

Pamela Perez, The Education Therapist™

PRINCIPLE # 1
KNOW THYSELF

ALL THE WONDERS THAT YOU SEEK IN LIFE ARE DEEP
INSIDE YOURSELF - REFLECT!

Writing down your thoughts is one way to get to know yourself. Describe something else that you can do to get to know yourself better.

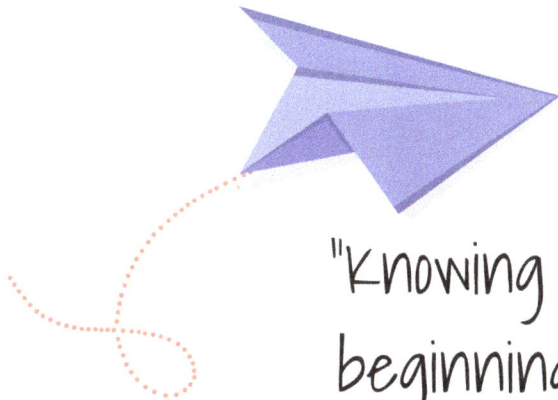

"Knowing yourself is the beginning of all wisdom."
-Aristotle

Pamela Perez, The Education Therapist™

This page is intentionally blank for additional vision items, journaling, or so that the principle on the reverse side can be laminated and used as a poster.

5 MINUTE JOURNALING

Reflections

TOP 3 GOOD THINGS TODAY:

O _____

O _____

O _____

WHAT EMOTIONS HAVE YOU FELT TODAY?

HOW WOULD YOU RATE THE DAY?

☆ ☆ ☆ ☆ ☆

WHAT INSPIRED YOU THE MOST TODAY?

3 THINGS I WISH FOR TOMORROW:

O _____

O _____

O _____

DOODLES AND DREAMS

date:

topic:

Dreams and Vision Goals

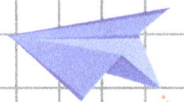

PRINCIPLE # 2
INCREASE YOUR LEVEL OF EMOTIONAL INTELLIGENCE

EMOTIONAL INTELLIGENCE IS THE ABILITY TO RECOGNIZE AND MANAGE YOUR EMOTIONS WELL. PEOPLE THAT ARE ALWAYS 'FLYING OFF THE HANDLE' WOULD BE CONSIDERED TO HAVE A LOWER LEVEL OF EMOTIONAL INTELLIGENCE.

Thoughts and feelings drive behavior. An emotion can be brought on by thinking a simple thought. Reflect on a time when you experienced a negative emotion based on something that you were thinking about just prior to feeling it. For example, you may feel angry after thinking that you were wronged by another person. How important is it for you to recognize your emotions prior to engaging in a negative behavior?

"Man is made by his belief.
As he believes, so is he."
-Johann Wolfgang Von Goethe

This page is intentionally blank for additional vision items, journaling, or so that the principle on the reverse side can be laminated and used as a poster.

5 MINUTE JOURNALING

Reflections

_____

_____

_____

_____

_____

_____

_____

_____

_____

_____

TOP 3 GOOD THINGS TODAY:

O _____

O _____

O _____

WHAT EMOTIONS HAVE YOU FELT TODAY?

HOW WOULD YOU RATE THE DAY?

☆ ☆ ☆ ☆ ☆

WHAT INSPIRED YOU THE MOST TODAY?

3 THINGS I WISH FOR TOMORROW:

O _____

O _____

O _____

DOODLES AND DREAMS

date:

topic:

Dreams and Vision Goals

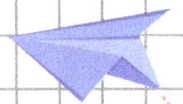

PRINCIPLE # 3
BEHAVIOR: OBEY AUTHORITY

Parents, elders, guardians, teachers, and law enforcement are put in place to protect you. It is always in your best interest to listen to their guidance.
(I think you might even live longer!)

Wisdom is most often given through the elders in our lives. For example, my Grandmother once told me to never spare expense on 2 things in life...

1. **Good shoes** (Because we are always on our feet.)
2. **Good mattress** (Because we sleep 1/3 of our lives.)

Reflect on an experience that you had when you did not listen to the wise counsel of an elder in your life.
What happened and what did you learn from the experience?

"Listen to your elder's advice, not because they are always right but because they have more experiences of being wrong."
-unknown

Pamela Perez, The Education Therapist™

This page is intentionally blank for additional vision items, journaling, or so that the principle on the reverse side can be laminated and used as a poster.

5 MINUTE JOURNALING

Reflections

TOP 3 GOOD THINGS TODAY:

O _____

O _____

O _____

WHAT EMOTIONS HAVE YOU FELT TODAY?

WHAT INSPIRED YOU THE MOST TODAY?

3 THINGS I WISH FOR TOMORROW:

O _____

O _____

O _____

HOW WOULD YOU RATE THE DAY?

☆ ☆ ☆ ☆ ☆

DOODLES AND DREAMS

date:

topic:

Dreams and Vision Goals

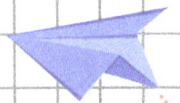

PRINCIPLE # 4
GIVE TO RECEIVE, SOW TO REAP

There is a universal principle that says, "If you give, you will receive." It is also called planting and harvesting. Just as the farmer does not get crops overnight, the rewards will take time. But if you are consistent in your planting and watering, you will reap what you sow.

Never forget that the entire universe is established upon fixed laws. Sowing and reaping is one of those inescapable laws.

Describe a time in your life when you gave something away only to find that you experienced a reward in doing so.

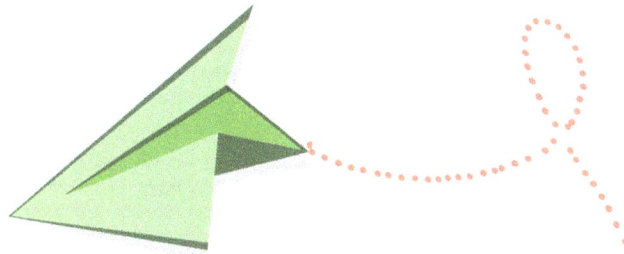

"No one has ever become poor by giving."
- The Diary of Anne Frank

Pamela Perez, The Education Therapist™

This page is intentionally blank for additional vision items, journaling, or so that
the principle on the reverse side can be laminated and used as a poster.

5 MINUTE JOURNALING

_____

_____

_____

_____

_____

_____

_____

_____

_____

_____

Reflections

TOP 3 GOOD THINGS TODAY:

O _____

O _____

O _____

WHAT EMOTIONS HAVE YOU FELT TODAY?

HOW WOULD YOU RATE THE DAY?

☆ ☆ ☆ ☆ ☆

WHAT INSPIRED YOU THE MOST TODAY?

3 THINGS I WISH FOR TOMORROW:

O _____

O _____

O _____

15

DOODLES AND DREAMS

date:

topic:

Dreams and Vision Goals

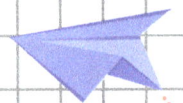

PRINCIPLE # 5
OBSERVE THE GOLDEN RULE

You have heard the saying, *"Treat others the way you would like to be treated."* This universal principle works by reciprocity—kind of like a boomerang. It means what you give out comes back to you, but it must begin with you. We cannot change others, but we hold the power to change ourselves.

When someone is angry, a kind word can be just what it takes to calm them down. **Give it a try!**

Always take a moment to put yourself in the shoes of others before you say or do something.

What specific way do you apply the "Golden Rule" in your life?

"If you contemplate the Golden Rule, it turns out to be an injunction to live by grace rather than by what you think other people deserve."
-Deepak Chopra

Pamela Perez, The Education Therapist™

This page is intentionally blank for additional vision items, journaling, or so that the principle on the reverse side can be laminated and used as a poster.

5 MINUTE JOURNALING

Reflections

_____
_____
_____
_____
_____
_____
_____
_____
_____
_____

TOP 3 GOOD THINGS TODAY:

O _____
O _____
O _____

WHAT EMOTIONS HAVE YOU FELT TODAY?

HOW WOULD YOU RATE THE DAY?

☆ ☆ ☆ ☆ ☆

WHAT INSPIRED YOU THE MOST TODAY?

3 THINGS I WISH FOR TOMORROW:

O _____
O _____
O _____

19

DOODLES AND DREAMS

date:

topic:

Dreams and Vision Goals

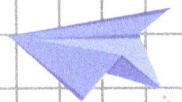

PRINCIPLE # 6

FOLLOW YOUR PASSION IN LIFE, AND IT WILL LEAD YOU TO YOUR PURPOSE

There is a saying that states, "If you do what you love to do, you will never work a day in your life." Why is this so? Because when you are doing what you love, it doesn't feel like work!

DO WHAT YOU LOVE!

Describe something that you are passionate about. How would following your passion help other people?

"Purpose is the reason you journey. Passion is the fire that lights the way."
-unknown

Pamela Perez, The Education Therapist™

This page is intentionally blank for additional vision items, journaling, or so that the principle on the reverse side can be laminated and used as a poster.

5 MINUTE JOURNALING

Reflections

TOP 3 GOOD THINGS TODAY:

O _____

O _____

O _____

WHAT EMOTIONS HAVE YOU FELT TODAY?

WHAT INSPIRED YOU THE MOST TODAY?

3 THINGS I WISH FOR TOMORROW:

O _____

O _____

O _____

HOW WOULD YOU RATE THE DAY?

☆ ☆ ☆ ☆ ☆

DOODLES AND DREAMS

date:

topic:

Dreams and Vision Goals

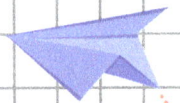

PRINCIPLE # 7
DISCOVER YOUR UNIQUE TALENTS AND STRENGTHS

Everyone has something that they are good at doing. Most of the time, this correlates with what you enjoy doing. Put in the time and effort to discover these talents, and they will serve you well in life!

Hint: Taking multiple assessments (aptitude tests, personality tests, career, and interest inventories) will help you in your quest to discover your strengths.

Describe 3 strengths/talents that you possess or things that you are good at doing.

"Talents are meant to be shared."
-Carol B. Thomas

This page is intentionally blank for additional vision items, journaling, or so that the principle on the reverse side can be laminated and used as a poster.

5 MINUTE JOURNALING

Reflections

TOP 3 GOOD THINGS TODAY:

O _____

O _____

O _____

WHAT EMOTIONS HAVE YOU FELT TODAY?

HOW WOULD YOU RATE THE DAY?

☆ ☆ ☆ ☆ ☆

WHAT INSPIRED YOU THE MOST TODAY?

3 THINGS I WISH FOR TOMORROW:

O _____

O _____

O _____

DOODLES AND DREAMS

date:

topic:

Dreams and Vision Goals

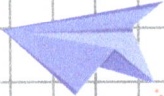

PRINCIPLE # 8
STAY FOCUSED

We are constantly mentally distracted by technology in today's world. To grow personally and achieve goals in life, you must be mentally focused.

There is a technique called "mindfulness," which simply means to be aware in the present. It can be very helpful to practice mindfulness to improve our ability to stay mentally focused.

There are studies that show how prayer and meditation can be beneficial to your health.
Why do you think this is so?

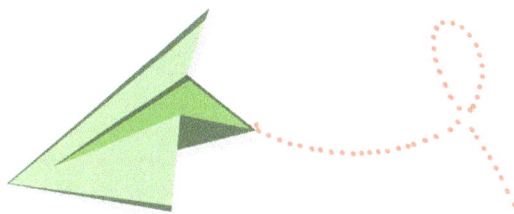

"If you want to be happy, do not dwell in the past. Do not worry about the future, focus on living fully in the present."
-Roy T. Bennett

Pamela Perez, The Education Therapist™

This page is intentionally blank for additional vision items, journaling, or so that the principle on the reverse side can be laminated and used as a poster.

5 MINUTE JOURNALING

Reflections

_____
_____
_____
_____
_____
_____
_____
_____
_____
_____

TOP 3 GOOD THINGS TODAY:

O _____
O _____
O _____

WHAT EMOTIONS HAVE YOU FELT TODAY?

WHAT INSPIRED YOU THE MOST TODAY?

HOW WOULD YOU RATE THE DAY?

☆ ☆ ☆ ☆ ☆

3 THINGS I WISH FOR TOMORROW:

O _____
O _____
O _____

31

DOODLES AND DREAMS

date:

topic:

Dreams and Vision Goals

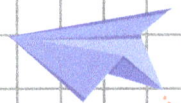

PRINCIPLE # 9
HAVE A VISION

For you to move forward in life, you must have a vision. A vision is something that you see for your future. Write it down, look at it often, think about it daily, and set small attainable goals toward the vision. Soon you will begin to look back and see how far you have progressed in your journey.

Remember these 2 things:

1. "Slow and steady wins the race," said the hare.

2. The path towards the vision is a journey, not a destination.

Why is it important for you to have a vision and set goals in life? Can you list a few of your goals, dreams, or visions?

"Vision without action is merely a dream. Action without vision just passes the time. Vision with action can change the world."
-Joel A. Barker

Pamela Perez, The Education Therapist™

This page is intentionally blank for additional vision items, journaling, or so that the principle on the reverse side can be laminated and used as a poster.

5 MINUTE JOURNALING

_____
_____
_____
_____
_____
_____
_____
_____
_____
_____
_____

Reflections

TOP 3 GOOD THINGS TODAY:

O _____
O _____
O _____

WHAT EMOTIONS HAVE YOU FELT TODAY?

HOW WOULD YOU RATE THE DAY?

☆ ☆ ☆ ☆ ☆

WHAT INSPIRED YOU THE MOST TODAY?

3 THINGS I WISH FOR TOMORROW:

O _____
O _____
O _____

35

DOODLES AND DREAMS

date:

topic:

Dreams and Vision Goals

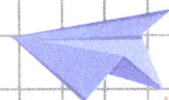

PRINCIPLE # 10
DO ONE THING AT A TIME

I once heard a story of a man who was paid $25,000 to help a factory owner increase his factory's level of production. The man said to the factory owner, "If I can tell you one thing that is guaranteed to increase your factory's productivity, what is it worth to you?" The factory owner replied, "If it is guaranteed to work, I will give you $25,000 right now."

The man told the factory owner to take out a sheet of paper and write down 5 things he wanted to accomplish today. The factory owner said to the man, "I don't understand how this will increase production in my factory?" The man said, "I promise that if you will do this daily and accomplish one thing at a time, you are guaranteed to greatly increase productivity. It never fails!" The factory owner thought about it for a second and then wrote the man a check for $25,000.

There is a term often used called "multitasking." Do you think that it is more or less effective than focusing on a single task at a time? Why?

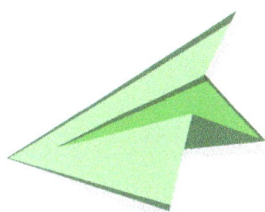

"Focus on being productive instead of busy."
-Tim Ferriss

Pamela Perez, The Education Therapist™

This page is intentionally blank for additional vision items, journaling, or so that
the principle on the reverse side can be laminated and used as a poster.

5 MINUTE JOURNALING

Reflections

TOP 3 GOOD THINGS TODAY:

O _____

O _____

O _____

WHAT EMOTIONS HAVE YOU FELT TODAY?

HOW WOULD YOU RATE THE DAY?

☆ ☆ ☆ ☆ ☆

WHAT INSPIRED YOU THE MOST TODAY?

3 THINGS I WISH FOR TOMORROW:

O _____

O _____

O _____

39

DOODLES AND DREAMS

date:

topic:

Dreams and Vision Goals

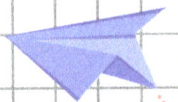

PRINCIPLE # 11
WATCH WHO YOU HANG AROUND

You become like those that you associate with in life. Look at the 5 people with whom you spend most of your time. There is a constant influence in life, and you must ask yourself if the people you associate with are of good character.

When people are in recovery from addiction, they are told that they must change 3 things in life: playthings, playgrounds, and playmates.

Behavior will not change if the people around you continue to negatively influence you.

Name or describe the 5 people closest to you and reflect on how these people are influencing your life. Are they positive or negative influences? Why?

"You are the average of the five people that you spend the most time with."
-Jim Rohn

Pamela Perez, The Education Therapist™

41

This page is intentionally blank for additional vision items, journaling, or so that the principle on the reverse side can be laminated and used as a poster.

5 MINUTE JOURNALING

_____
_____
_____
_____
_____
_____

Reflections

_____
_____
_____
_____

TOP 3 GOOD THINGS TODAY:

O _____

O _____

O _____

WHAT EMOTIONS HAVE YOU FELT TODAY?

HOW WOULD YOU RATE THE DAY?

☆ ☆ ☆ ☆ ☆

WHAT INSPIRED YOU THE MOST TODAY?

3 THINGS I WISH FOR TOMORROW:

O _____

O _____

O _____

43

DOODLES AND DREAMS

date:

topic:

Dreams and Vision Goals

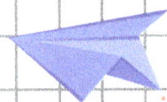

PRINCIPLE # 12
PERSONAL GROWTH IS THE KEY TO LIFE

We cannot change anyone but ourselves; therefore, we must always strive for personal growth.

There are 3 things required for us to grow:
1. Awareness of ourselves
2. Personal responsibility
3. Humility

Why do you think that "awareness" is so important to personal growth?

"The greatest day in your life and mine is when we take total responsibility for our attitudes. That's the day we truly grow up."
-John C. Maxwell

Pamela Perez, The Education Therapist™

This page is intentionally blank for additional vision items, journaling, or so that the principle on the reverse side can be laminated and used as a poster.

5 MINUTE JOURNALING

Reflections

TOP 3 GOOD THINGS TODAY:

O _____
O _____
O _____

WHAT EMOTIONS HAVE YOU FELT TODAY?

HOW WOULD YOU RATE THE DAY?

☆ ☆ ☆ ☆ ☆

WHAT INSPIRED YOU THE MOST TODAY?

3 THINGS I WISH FOR TOMORROW:

O _____
O _____
O _____

47

DOODLES AND DREAMS

date:

topic:

Dreams and Vision Goals

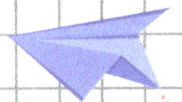

PRINCIPLE # 13
TAKE CARE OF YOUR BODY

You only have this one body in life, take care of it and it will take care of you.

Your body is not much different than your car. If you want your car to last a long time, you must provide continuous maintenance. You must regularly change the oil and other fluids and keep it clean. You can't abuse your car and expect it to perform well in return.

Here are 5 simple things that you can do regularly to keep your body running smoothly:

1. Eat less sugar and more fruits and veggies.
2. Get at least 8 hours of sleep nightly.
3. Avoid toxins (pesticides, drugs, etc.).
4. Drink more water.
5. Practice Mindfulness.

List 5 things that you are doing right now to take care of your physical body.

What things can you do to further improve your physical health?

"Self-care is giving the world the best of you, instead of the rest of you."
-Katie Reed

This page is intentionally blank for additional vision items, journaling, or so that
the principle on the reverse side can be laminated and used as a poster.

5 MINUTE JOURNALING

Reflections

_____

_____

_____

_____

_____

_____

_____

_____

_____

TOP 3 GOOD THINGS TODAY:

O _____

O _____

O _____

WHAT EMOTIONS HAVE YOU FELT TODAY?

HOW WOULD YOU RATE THE DAY?

☆ ☆ ☆ ☆ ☆

WHAT INSPIRED YOU THE MOST TODAY?

3 THINGS I WISH FOR TOMORROW:

O _____

O _____

O _____

51

DOODLES AND DREAMS

date:

topic:

Dreams and Vision Goals

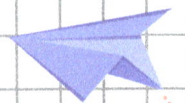

PRINCIPLE # 14
IF YOU WANT FRIENDS, BE FRIENDLY

Do you ever notice how it makes you feel to receive a compliment? It feels great!

Therefore, if a compliment is warranted, don't hold on to it, give it away!

You may never realize the impact your friendship has on another person. Here are some tips for gaining friends:

1. Join a group or team.
2. Give compliments often (written or spoken).
3. Say hello first.

Our environment is often a reflection of what is going on inside of us. A smile will often generate a smile from others. What are 3 things you can do to build better friendships or show friendliness to others?

"I've learned that people will forget what you said, people will forget what you did, but people will never forget how you made them feel."
-Maya Angelou

Pamela Perez, The Education Therapist™

This page is intentionally blank for additional vision items, journaling, or so that
the principle on the reverse side can be laminated and used as a poster.

5 MINUTE JOURNALING

Reflections

_____

_____

_____

_____

_____

_____

_____

_____

_____

_____

TOP 3 GOOD THINGS TODAY:

O _____

O _____

O _____

WHAT EMOTIONS HAVE YOU FELT TODAY?

HOW WOULD YOU RATE THE DAY?

☆ ☆ ☆ ☆ ☆

WHAT INSPIRED YOU THE MOST TODAY?

3 THINGS I WISH FOR TOMORROW:

O _____

O _____

O _____

55

DOODLES AND DREAMS

date:

topic:

Dreams and Vision Goals

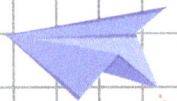

PRINCIPLE # 15
LAUGH DAILY

Have you ever heard that laughter is like medicine? Studies have shown that it helps to heal sickness and disease. It does this by supporting a healthy immune system, relieving stress, and increasing certain neurotransmitters like dopamine. Laughter suggested dose: Give yourself a minimum of one belly laugh per day and it may help to keep the doctor away.

What things can you do to increase the fun and laughter in your life?

"Laughter is the best medicine in the world."
-Milton Berle

This page is intentionally blank for additional vision items, journaling, or so that the principle on the reverse side can be laminated and used as a poster.

5 MINUTE JOURNALING

Reflections

TOP 3 GOOD THINGS TODAY:

○ _____

○ _____

○ _____

WHAT EMOTIONS HAVE YOU FELT TODAY?

HOW WOULD YOU RATE THE DAY?

☆ ☆ ☆ ☆ ☆

WHAT INSPIRED YOU THE MOST TODAY?

3 THINGS I WISH FOR TOMORROW:

○ _____

○ _____

○ _____

DOODLES AND DREAMS

date:

topic:

Dreams and Vision Goals

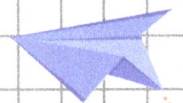

PRINCIPLE # 16
LEARN RELAXATION TECHNIQUES

Since stress is unavoidable in life, you need to learn a few helpful ways to deal with stress when it comes. There are numerous ways in which you can teach yourself to slow down and relax.

Here are a few helpful relaxation tips:
1. Mindfulness
2. Deep Stretches
3. Deep Breathing
4. Meditation & Prayer
5. Journaling

What are some positive things that you can do to deal with stressful events in your life?

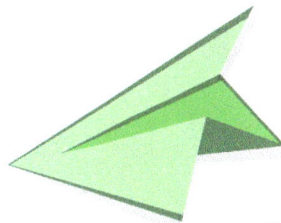

"Almost everything will work again if you unplug it for a few minutes...including you."
-Anne Lamott

Pamela Perez, The Education Therapist™

This page is intentionally blank for additional vision items, journaling, or so that the principle on the reverse side can be laminated and used as a poster.

5 MINUTE JOURNALING

Reflections

_____
_____
_____
_____
_____
_____
_____
_____
_____
_____

TOP 3 GOOD THINGS TODAY:

O _____
O _____
O _____

WHAT EMOTIONS HAVE YOU FELT TODAY?

HOW WOULD YOU RATE THE DAY?

☆ ☆ ☆ ☆ ☆

WHAT INSPIRED YOU THE MOST TODAY?

3 THINGS I WISH FOR TOMORROW:

O _____
O _____
O _____

63

DOODLES AND DREAMS

date:

topic:

Dreams and Vision Goals

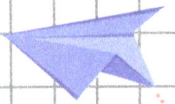

PRINCIPLE # 17
STRETCH

Do you ever notice that animals stretch instinctively? Nobody had to teach a dog or cat to stretch. It appears that it must be beneficial for them in some way.

Now you try it! It feels pretty good, right?

This is because your muscles and tendons can get very tight and it helps to loosen them up. People who take regular deep stretch and yoga classes also realize great benefits.

Make this a daily habit and your body will thank you.

How often do you stretch your body?
How can you easily incorporate this into your daily routine?

"You are only as young as your spine is flexible."
—Joseph Pilates

This page is intentionally blank for additional vision items, journaling, or so that the principle on the reverse side can be laminated and used as a poster.

5 MINUTE JOURNALING

Reflections

_____
_____
_____
_____
_____
_____

_____
_____
_____
_____
_____

TOP 3 GOOD THINGS TODAY:

O _____

O _____

O _____

WHAT EMOTIONS HAVE YOU FELT TODAY?

HOW WOULD YOU RATE THE DAY?

☆ ☆ ☆ ☆ ☆

WHAT INSPIRED YOU THE MOST TODAY?

3 THINGS I WISH FOR TOMORROW:

O _____

O _____

O _____

DOODLES AND DREAMS

date:

topic:

Dreams and Vision Goals

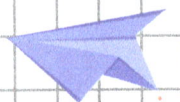

PRINCIPLE # 18
VOLUNTEER TO HELP THE NEEDY

There are always going to be those that are less fortunate than you.

Always remember that it is better to give than to receive and if you have the ability, it's your duty to give back to your fellow man. You never know if you will be on the receiving end one day.

If for no other reason, give to the needy because it feels good and it's good for your mental health.

In what ways do you volunteer to help those less fortunate than you?

How can you increase your level of giving to others?

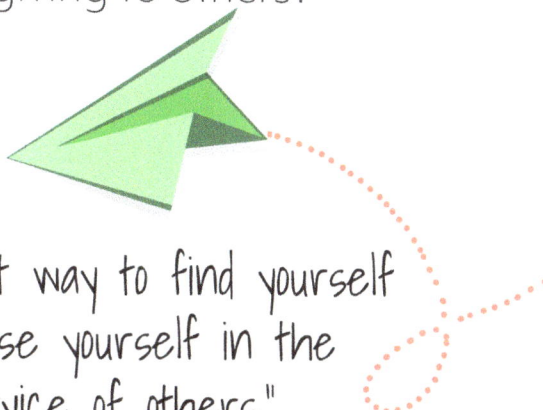

"The best way to find yourself is to lose yourself in the service of others."
-Mahatma Gandhi

Pamela Perez, The Education Therapist™

This page is intentionally blank for additional vision items, journaling, or so that
the principle on the reverse side can be laminated and used as a poster.

5 MINUTE JOURNALING

Reflections

_____
_____
_____
_____
_____
_____
_____
_____
_____
_____
_____

TOP 3 GOOD THINGS TODAY:

O _____
O _____
O _____

WHAT EMOTIONS HAVE YOU FELT TODAY?

HOW WOULD YOU RATE THE DAY?

☆ ☆ ☆ ☆ ☆

WHAT INSPIRED YOU THE MOST TODAY?

3 THINGS I WISH FOR TOMORROW:

O _____
O _____
O _____

71

DOODLES AND DREAMS

date:

topic:

Dreams and Vision Goals

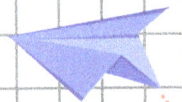

PRINCIPLE # 19
THERE ARE NO MISTAKES, JUST LESSONS

Life lessons are often disguised as mistakes and are meant to teach us something valuable. If you fail to learn from a lesson, you may have to repeat the process a few times before moving onward.

Life is full of patterns and cycles that can keep you stuck. This is an opportunity to analyze and self-examine. If you are tired of repeating old patterns, begin by working to change old beliefs.

Are you able to learn from your own mistakes? Describe a lesson that you learned from making a poor choice.

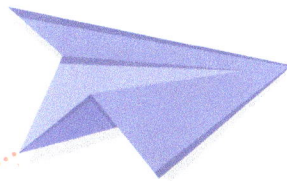

"It's not how we make mistakes, but how we correct them that defines us."
-Rachel Wolchin

This page is intentionally blank for additional vision items, journaling, or so that
the principle on the reverse side can be laminated and used as a poster.

5 MINUTE JOURNALING

Reflections

_____
_____
_____
_____
_____
_____
_____
_____
_____

TOP 3 GOOD THINGS TODAY:

O _____
O _____
O _____

WHAT EMOTIONS HAVE YOU FELT TODAY?

WHAT INSPIRED YOU THE MOST TODAY?

HOW WOULD YOU RATE THE DAY?

☆ ☆ ☆ ☆ ☆

3 THINGS I WISH FOR TOMORROW:

O _____
O _____
O _____

DOODLES AND DREAMS

date:

topic:

Dreams and Vision Goals

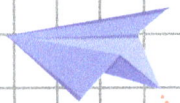

PRINCIPLE # 20
WATCH YOUR WORDS

Words are like seeds in the ground, they will produce fruit.

If someone says that words do not matter, they fail to understand the power of words. Words are like a rudder that steers the ship. If you pay attention to your words, you will see the direction that your ship is taking.

Words have the power to bring about hope and restoration just as they have the power to bring about despair and destruction.

Choose your words carefully, and they will help guide you along the path of life.

In what ways are the words that you are speaking directing your life?

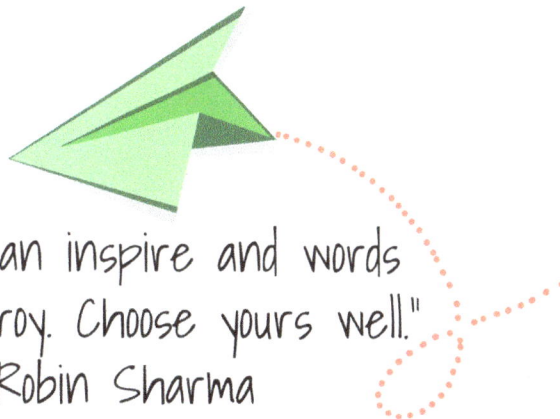

"Words can inspire and words can destroy. Choose yours well."
-Robin Sharma

This page is intentionally blank for additional vision items, journaling, or so that the principle on the reverse side can be laminated and used as a poster.

5 MINUTE JOURNALING

_____
_____
_____
_____
_____
_____

_____
_____
_____
_____
_____

Reflections

TOP 3 GOOD THINGS TODAY:

O _____
O _____
O _____

WHAT EMOTIONS HAVE YOU FELT TODAY?

HOW WOULD YOU RATE THE DAY?

☆ ☆ ☆ ☆ ☆

WHAT INSPIRED YOU THE MOST TODAY?

3 THINGS I WISH FOR TOMORROW:

O _____
O _____
O _____

DOODLES AND DREAMS

date:

topic:

Dreams and Vision Goals

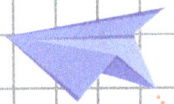

PRINCIPLE # 21
WALK IN LOVE AND KINDNESS

You probably know what it means to be kind to someone, but do you know what it means to love someone?

Love is often mistaken for the romantic love that we all want to feel in life. On the other hand, there are other forms of love but the greatest love of all is self-sacrificing.

Examine this definition of love and describe ways in which you can improve on demonstrating love toward others in your own life.

"Love is patient, love is kind. Love does not envy, it does not boast, it is not proud. It doesn't dishonor others, it is not self-seeking, it is not easily angered, it keeps no record of wrongs. It does not find pleasure in evil but in truth. Love always protects, trusts, hopes, and perseveres."

-Holy Bible, New International Version

Pamela Perez, The Education Therapist™

This page is intentionally blank for additional vision items, journaling, or so that the principle on the reverse side can be laminated and used as a poster.

5 MINUTE JOURNALING

_____
_____
_____
_____
_____
_____

Reflections

_____
_____
_____
_____
_____

TOP 3 GOOD THINGS TODAY:

O _____
O _____
O _____

WHAT EMOTIONS HAVE YOU FELT TODAY?

WHAT INSPIRED YOU THE MOST TODAY?

3 THINGS I WISH FOR TOMORROW:

O _____
O _____
O _____

HOW WOULD YOU RATE THE DAY?

☆ ☆ ☆ ☆ ☆

DOODLES AND DREAMS

date:

topic:

Dreams and Vision Goals

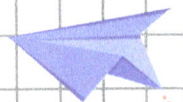

PRINCIPLE # 22
EXPRESS YOUR FEELINGS

Most people think of emotions in terms of negative and positive. Psychology has defined various emotions like anger, sadness, happiness, and fear. On the other hand, there are only two real sources from which emotions arise. These sources are love and fear.

It is vital that you learn to express yourself in life. Bottled emotions can cause all kinds of psychological and physical problems. Have you heard the expression, "getting it off my chest?" Sometimes you need to talk to someone and release the emotional burden within.

Remember: Emotions are like a pressure cooker, there must be a release valve, or they will explode!

Describe a few things that you can do to express your anger in a healthy way without hurting yourself or others.

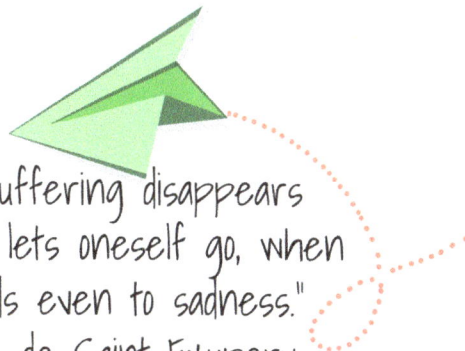

"One's suffering disappears when one lets oneself go, when one yields even to sadness."
-Antoine de Saint-Exupery

This page is intentionally blank for additional vision items, journaling, or so that the principle on the reverse side can be laminated and used as a poster.

5 MINUTE JOURNALING

Reflections

_____

_____

_____

_____

_____

_____

_____

_____

_____

_____

_____

TOP 3 GOOD THINGS TODAY:

O _____

O _____

O _____

WHAT EMOTIONS HAVE YOU FELT TODAY?

HOW WOULD YOU RATE THE DAY?

☆ ☆ ☆ ☆ ☆

WHAT INSPIRED YOU THE MOST TODAY?

3 THINGS I WISH FOR TOMORROW:

O _____

O _____

O _____ 87

DOODLES AND DREAMS

date:

topic:

Dreams and Vision Goals

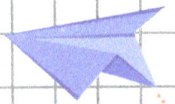

PRINCIPLE # 23
BE SOCIAL

There have been several studies that show how our social life correlates with our health, both mental and physical.

People who are depressed tend to isolate themselves for various reasons. The problem is that the tendency to isolate makes depression worse. Sometimes you must force yourself to be around others. It may seem difficult at first, but you will be glad that you made the initial effort.

It is never good for anyone to be alone. We are social beings that were created to love and be loved.

Name a few things that you can do to have a more positive social life.

"Humans are social beings, and we are happier, and better, when connected to others."
-Paul Bloom

Pamela Perez, The Education Therapist™

This page is intentionally blank for additional vision items, journaling, or so that
the principle on the reverse side can be laminated and used as a poster.

5 MINUTE JOURNALING

Reflections

_____

_____

_____

_____

_____

_____

_____

_____

_____

TOP 3 GOOD THINGS TODAY:

O _____

O _____

O _____

WHAT EMOTIONS HAVE YOU FELT TODAY?

WHAT INSPIRED YOU THE MOST TODAY?

3 THINGS I WISH FOR TOMORROW:

O _____

O _____

O _____

HOW WOULD YOU RATE THE DAY?

☆ ☆ ☆ ☆ ☆

91

DOODLES AND DREAMS

date:

topic:

Dreams and Vision Goals

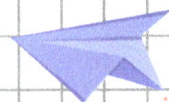

PRINCIPLE # 24
AVOID NEGATIVITY

Have you ever been around certain people that constantly complain and talk negatively? Does this make you feel uplifted or drained, or are you a part of the equation?

When you are continually in negative environments, you must ask yourself, "Why?" Are you contributing to this negativity? Are you drawn to this negativity? Is there something that you need to address?

Whatever you feed grows. Ask yourself, "Am I feeding on positivity or negativity?" If you want to think, feel and act positively, the change starts with you!

How can you turn a negative situation or event into a more positive one?

"There are so many great things in life; why dwell on negativity?"
-Zendaya

Pamela Perez, The Education Therapist™

This page is intentionally blank for additional vision items, journaling, or so that the principle on the reverse side can be laminated and used as a poster.

5 MINUTE JOURNALING

Reflections

_____

_____

_____

_____

_____

_____

_____

_____

_____

_____

_____

TOP 3 GOOD THINGS TODAY:

O _____

O _____

O _____

WHAT EMOTIONS HAVE YOU FELT TODAY?

HOW WOULD YOU RATE THE DAY?

☆ ☆ ☆ ☆ ☆

WHAT INSPIRED YOU THE MOST TODAY?

3 THINGS I WISH FOR TOMORROW:

O _____

O _____

O _____

95

DOODLES AND DREAMS

date:

topic:

Dreams and Vision Goals

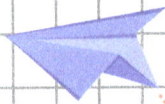

PRINCIPLE # 25
FEED ON POSITIVITY

Do you ever wonder why watching a horror movie can sometimes cause nightmares?

It is because the mind is heavily influenced by what it is exposed to externally.

We are continually affected by the five senses: what we see, hear, smell, touch, and taste. If we want to feel good mentally, we must focus on positivity in our environment.

Ask yourself these questions:
    Do I listen to positive uplifting music?
    Do I watch positive uplifting movies/videos?

What types of movies, books, music, etc., do you regularly focus your mind upon?

Can you think of a time when you watched a certain type of movie and had a dream about it afterwards?

"I always like a good song: puts me in a good mood."
-Waris Ahluwalia

Pamela Perez, The Education Therapist™

This page is intentionally blank for additional vision items, journaling, or so that the principle on the reverse side can be laminated and used as a poster.

5 MINUTE JOURNALING

Reflections

TOP 3 GOOD THINGS TODAY:

O _____

O _____

O _____

WHAT EMOTIONS HAVE YOU FELT TODAY?

HOW WOULD YOU RATE THE DAY?

☆ ☆ ☆ ☆ ☆

WHAT INSPIRED YOU THE MOST TODAY?

3 THINGS I WISH FOR TOMORROW:

O _____

O _____

O _____

DOODLES AND DREAMS

date:

topic:

Dreams and Vision Goals

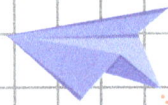

PRINCIPLE # 26
FOCUS ON BEAUTY

There is beauty all around you if you will pay attention. The more beauty that you focus upon, the more that you will draw beautiful things to you.

The following are a few examples of the beautiful things in life to focus your mind upon:

1. A sunset
2. A sunrise
3. Mountains
4. Beaches
5. Babies
6. Puppies
7. Flowers

What other beautiful things can you focus upon in your life?

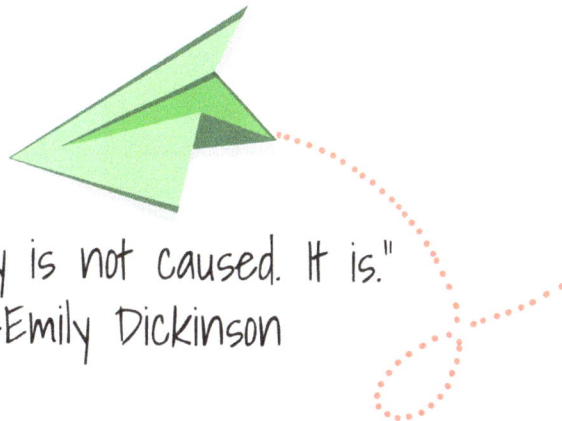

"Beauty is not caused. It is."
-Emily Dickinson

Pamela Perez, The Education Therapist™

This page is intentionally blank for additional vision items, journaling, or so that the principle on the reverse side can be laminated and used as a poster.

5 MINUTE JOURNALING

Reflections

TOP 3 GOOD THINGS TODAY:

O _____

O _____

O _____

WHAT EMOTIONS HAVE YOU FELT TODAY?

WHAT INSPIRED YOU THE MOST TODAY?

HOW WOULD YOU RATE THE DAY?

☆ ☆ ☆ ☆ ☆

3 THINGS I WISH FOR TOMORROW:

O _____

O _____

O _____

103

DOODLES AND DREAMS

date:

topic:

Dreams and Vision Goals

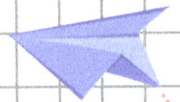

PRINCIPLE # 27
BE SUPPORTIVE

We are all connected, and we need one another. Be a supportive friend to those that need a listening ear or a supportive hug.

We have family and friends so that we are not alone when we need help. There will always be a need for support in your life, so be that support for someone else until you need it for yourself.

In what ways are you a support to your family members or friends?

"Anything is possible when you have the right people there to support you."
-Misty Copeland

This page is intentionally blank for additional vision items, journaling, or so that the principle on the reverse side can be laminated and used as a poster.

5 MINUTE JOURNALING

_____
_____
_____
_____
_____
_____
_____
_____
_____
_____
_____

Reflections

TOP 3 GOOD THINGS TODAY:

O _____

O _____

O _____

WHAT EMOTIONS HAVE YOU FELT TODAY?

HOW WOULD YOU RATE THE DAY?

☆ ☆ ☆ ☆ ☆

WHAT INSPIRED YOU THE MOST TODAY?

3 THINGS I WISH FOR TOMORROW:

O _____

O _____

O _____

107

DOODLES AND DREAMS

date:

topic:

Dreams and Vision Goals

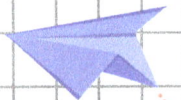

PRINCIPLE # 28
STUDY SUCCESSFUL PEOPLE AND IMITATE THEM

If you set a goal and see other people who have already achieved that goal, find out how they did it. Sometimes you can research their steps of actions and sometimes you can ask them directly.

If you want to be a successful basketball player, you must first study and follow those that have become successful at the game.

You will find that not only was skill involved but also practice, practice, and more practice!

Think of a person that you greatly admire, living or dead. What types of behavior and habits did they portray?

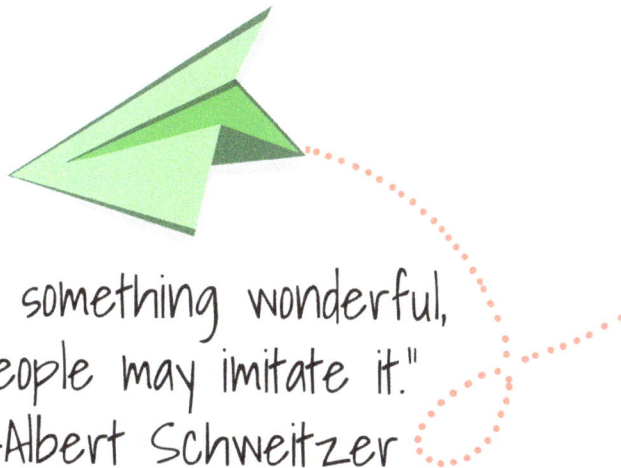

"Do something wonderful, people may imitate it."
-Albert Schweitzer

Pamela Perez, The Education Therapist™

This page is intentionally blank for additional vision items, journaling, or so that the principle on the reverse side can be laminated and used as a poster.

5 MINUTE JOURNALING

Reflections

_____

_____

_____

_____

_____

_____

_____

_____

_____

_____

TOP 3 GOOD THINGS TODAY:

O _____

O _____

O _____

WHAT EMOTIONS HAVE YOU FELT TODAY?

HOW WOULD YOU RATE THE DAY?

☆ ☆ ☆ ☆ ☆

WHAT INSPIRED YOU THE MOST TODAY?

3 THINGS I WISH FOR TOMORROW:

O _____

O _____

O _____

DOODLES AND DREAMS

date:

topic:

Dreams and Vision Goals

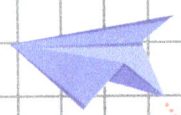

PRINCIPLE # 29
FORGIVE OFTEN AND DON'T HOLD GRUDGES

If you only remember one principle in life, remember this one!

When you hold a grudge and fail to forgive someone or something, you become tied to that person or thing. It is a stronger cord than steel, and it will affect your entire life until you release it.

It is important that you learn to let things roll off you easily and see others through the eyes of love. This may not always be easy, but the sooner you learn to walk in forgiveness, the happier you will be in life.

How important do you think that forgiveness is in life? Can you think of a time when it was very difficult to forgive an offense? How did it affect your life?

"To forgive is to set a prisoner free and discover that the prisoner was you."
-Lewis B. Smedes

Pamela Perez, The Education Therapist™

This page is intentionally blank for additional vision items, journaling, or so that
the principle on the reverse side can be laminated and used as a poster.

5 MINUTE JOURNALING

Reflections

TOP 3 GOOD THINGS TODAY:

O

O

O

WHAT EMOTIONS HAVE YOU FELT TODAY?

HOW WOULD YOU RATE THE DAY?

☆ ☆ ☆ ☆ ☆

WHAT INSPIRED YOU THE MOST TODAY?

3 THINGS I WISH FOR TOMORROW:

O

O

O

DOODLES AND DREAMS

date:

topic:

Dreams and Vision Goals

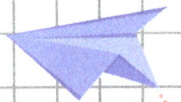

PRINCIPLE # 30
SMILE OFTEN

A smile is a powerful force in the world. Some have even said that it can cure an ailment. Did you know that it takes less muscles to smile than it does to frown?

A smile is one of those things that can produce joy. Usually when others see you smile, they tend to smile themselves. Smiles go out into the world to reflect happiness in others. The joy that you seek starts within you!

Try smiling at strangers and see what happens.

How often do you smile on a daily basis? Think of ways to increase those daily smiles in your life.

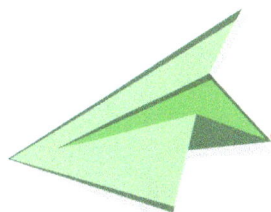

"Smile, it's free therapy."
-Douglas Horton

Pamela Perez, The Education Therapist™

This page is intentionally blank for additional vision items, journaling, or so that the principle on the reverse side can be laminated and used as a poster.

5 MINUTE JOURNALING

Reflections

_____

TOP 3 GOOD THINGS TODAY:

O _____

O _____

O _____

WHAT EMOTIONS HAVE YOU FELT TODAY?

HOW WOULD YOU RATE THE DAY?

☆ ☆ ☆ ☆ ☆

WHAT INSPIRED YOU THE MOST TODAY?

3 THINGS I WISH FOR TOMORROW:

O _____

O _____

O _____

DOODLES AND DREAMS

date:

topic:

Dreams and Vision Goals

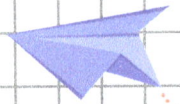

PRINCIPLE # 31
TRUST BRINGS HEALING

Just as love and joy can come from relationships, so does pain and betrayal.

The lesson to learn is that both hurt and healing can come from relationships.

Therefore, it is not in our best interest to avoid intimacy in relationships.

Sometimes the only way to heal is through a relationship, whether it be through a family member, friend, mate, or our Creator.

Don't ever discount the power of relationships because everything in life is always about relationships! You will find that TRUST is a major part of the relationship equation.

Why is trust so important in relationships? How can you build trust in your own relationships with others?

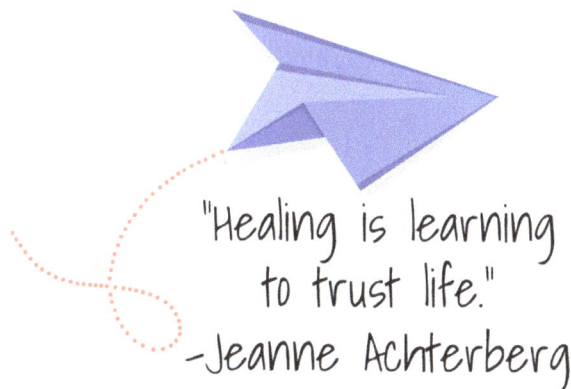

"Healing is learning to trust life."
-Jeanne Achterberg

This page is intentionally blank for additional vision items, journaling, or so that the principle on the reverse side can be laminated and used as a poster.

5 MINUTE JOURNALING

Reflections

TOP 3 GOOD THINGS TODAY:

O _____

O _____

O _____

WHAT EMOTIONS HAVE YOU FELT TODAY?

HOW WOULD YOU RATE THE DAY?

☆ ☆ ☆ ☆ ☆

WHAT INSPIRED YOU THE MOST TODAY?

3 THINGS I WISH FOR TOMORROW:

O _____

O _____

O _____

123

DOODLES AND DREAMS

date:

topic:

Dreams and Vision Goals

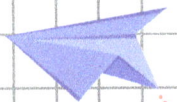

PRINCIPLE # 32
TAKE PERSONAL RESPONSIBILITY

We all must take personal responsibility for our thoughts, emotions, words, and actions. If you go through life avoiding personal responsibility, you will have many troubles.

What happens if we fail to take personal responsibility? We live out of the "victim mentality" which is always seeking to blame outside influences.

When we live out of the "victim mentality," we tend to look for payment from others. This keeps us making excuses and never growing beyond our current state.

In order to grow, we all must take personal responsibility for our thoughts, words, and actions. In what ways can you improve on taking personal responsibility for your behavior at home and at school?

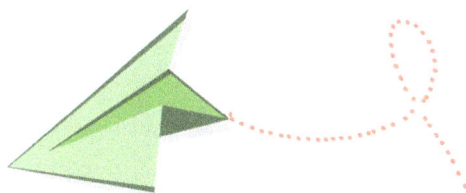

"I am not what happened to me,
I am what I choose to become."
-Carl Gustav Jung

Pamela Perez, The Education Therapist™

This page is intentionally blank for additional vision items, journaling, or so that the principle on the reverse side can be laminated and used as a poster.

5 MINUTE JOURNALING

Reflections

TOP 3 GOOD THINGS TODAY:

O _____

O _____

O _____

WHAT EMOTIONS HAVE YOU FELT TODAY?

HOW WOULD YOU RATE THE DAY?

☆ ☆ ☆ ☆ ☆

WHAT INSPIRED YOU THE MOST TODAY?

3 THINGS I WISH FOR TOMORROW:

O _____

O _____

O _____

DOODLES AND DREAMS

date:

topic:

Dreams and Vision Goals

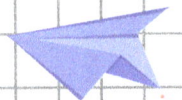

PRINCIPLE # 33
AVOID BLAME

There is a saying that, "Hurt people hurt people."

Along with taking personal responsibility comes avoiding putting the blame on others. You can't do one without the other. Let's face it, we all are challenged not to blame others for things in life.

Human beings hurt each other, sometimes intentionally and sometimes unintentionally. The problem exists when we fail to recognize the hurt inside of others. If someone is always angry, they are hurting.

Think of some negative situation that occurred at home or school. In what way did you blame the other party for something that may not have been their fault?

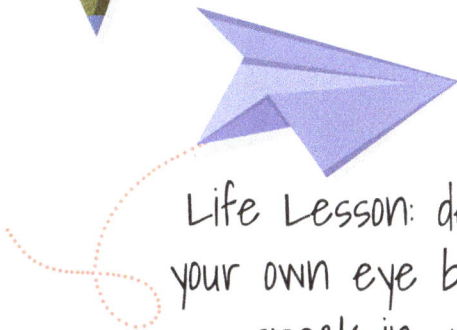

Life Lesson: deal with the plank in your own eye before focusing on the speck in your brother's eye.

Pamela Perez, The Education Therapist™

This page is intentionally blank for additional vision items, journaling, or so that the principle on the reverse side can be laminated and used as a poster.

5 MINUTE JOURNALING

Reflections

_____
_____
_____
_____
_____
_____
_____
_____
_____

TOP 3 GOOD THINGS TODAY:

O _____
O _____
O _____

WHAT EMOTIONS HAVE YOU FELT TODAY?

HOW WOULD YOU RATE THE DAY?

☆ ☆ ☆ ☆ ☆

WHAT INSPIRED YOU THE MOST TODAY?

3 THINGS I WISH FOR TOMORROW:

O _____
O _____
O _____

131

DOODLES AND DREAMS

date:

topic:

Dreams and Vision Goals

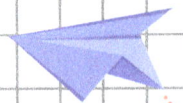

PRINCIPLE # 34
CHANGE YOUR THINKING
CHANGE YOUR LIFE

Don't ever underestimate the power of a thought. There is an order to life, and thoughts are the seeds of creativity. Meditate often on the following:

I am careful to choose my thoughts; they become my words.

I am careful to choose my words; they become my actions.

I am careful to choose my actions; they become my habits.

I am careful to choose my habits; they become my character.

I am careful to choose my character; it will determine my destiny.

In what ways can a thought produce something tangible in your life?

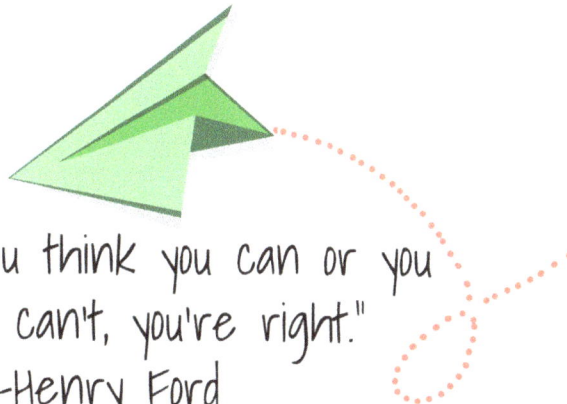

"Whether you think you can or you think you can't, you're right."
-Henry Ford

Pamela Perez, The Education Therapist™

This page is intentionally blank for additional vision items, journaling, or so that the principle on the reverse side can be laminated and used as a poster.

5 MINUTE JOURNALING

Reflections

TOP 3 GOOD THINGS TODAY:

O _____

O _____

O _____

WHAT EMOTIONS HAVE YOU FELT TODAY?

HOW WOULD YOU RATE THE DAY?

☆ ☆ ☆ ☆ ☆

WHAT INSPIRED YOU THE MOST TODAY?

3 THINGS I WISH FOR TOMORROW:

O _____

O _____

O _____

DOODLES AND DREAMS

date:

topic:

Dreams and vision goals

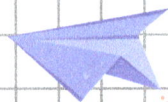

PRINCIPLE # 35
HONESTY IS THE BEST POLICY

Honesty also means integrity. People with integrity are honorable people. They speak truth and their words bless their lives.

We should always speak the truth in love although it may not always be popular. If you stand up for what is right and speak the truth in all things, you will be rewarded.

Being dishonest only breeds more dishonesty.

Being honest in situations at home or school is not being a "snitch." Describe a time that you were accused of being a "snitch" although deep inside, you knew it was the right thing to do.

"The greatest advantage to speaking the truth is that you don't have to remember what you said."
-unknown

Pamela Perez, The Education Therapist™

This page is intentionally blank for additional vision items, journaling, or so that the principle on the reverse side can be laminated and used as a poster.

5 MINUTE JOURNALING

_____

_____

_____

_____

_____

_____

_____

_____

_____

_____

_____

Reflections

TOP 3 GOOD THINGS TODAY:

O _____

O _____

O _____

WHAT EMOTIONS HAVE YOU FELT TODAY?

HOW WOULD YOU RATE THE DAY?

☆ ☆ ☆ ☆ ☆

WHAT INSPIRED YOU THE MOST TODAY?

3 THINGS I WISH FOR TOMORROW:

O _____

O _____

O _____

139

DOODLES AND DREAMS

date:

topic:

Dreams and vision goals

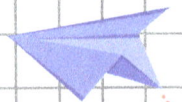

PRINCIPLE # 36
GREATNESS REQUIRES HUMILITY

Pride is the opposite of humility and will come before a fall. If you wish to be great, you must first learn how to be humble.

The way up begins at the bottom. Any great structure was first built upon a solid foundation from the ground. Consider the following:

Honor is given to people who walk in true humility. Identify 2 famous people in history that portrayed great humility.
What did they accomplish for mankind?

"Do you wish to rise?
Begin by descending. You plan
a tower that will pierce the clouds?
Lay first the foundation of humility."
- St Augustine

Pamela Perez, The Education Therapist™

This page is intentionally blank for additional vision items, journaling, or so that the principle on the reverse side can be laminated and used as a poster.

5 MINUTE JOURNALING

_____

_____

_____

_____

_____

_____

_____

_____

_____

_____

_____

Reflections

TOP 3 GOOD THINGS TODAY:

O _____

O _____

O _____

WHAT EMOTIONS HAVE YOU FELT TODAY?

HOW WOULD YOU RATE THE DAY?

☆ ☆ ☆ ☆ ☆

WHAT INSPIRED YOU THE MOST TODAY?

3 THINGS I WISH FOR TOMORROW:

O _____

O _____

O _____

143

DOODLES AND DREAMS

date:

topic:

Dreams and Vision Goals

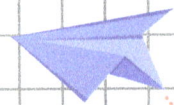

PRINCIPLE # 37
GRATITUDE IS MAGICAL

Research shows that there are numerous benefits of practicing gratitude, for us both mentally and physically.

The key is being able to see the good in everything.

Often, the greatest gains come out of the greatest trials and hardship, producing perseverance and character. Learn to be grateful in all things for you don't always see the greater outcome.

Name 5 things that you are most grateful for in life right now. Why?

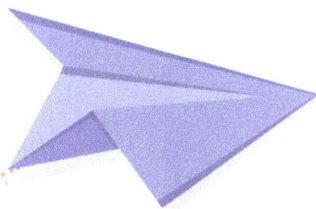

"When I started counting my blessings, my whole life turned around."
- Willie Nelson

This page is intentionally blank for additional vision items, journaling, or so that the principle on the reverse side can be laminated and used as a poster.

5 MINUTE JOURNALING

Reflections

_____

_____

_____

_____

_____

_____

_____

_____

_____

_____

_____

_____

TOP 3 GOOD THINGS TODAY:

O _____

O _____

O _____

WHAT EMOTIONS HAVE YOU FELT TODAY?

WHAT INSPIRED YOU THE MOST TODAY?

HOW WOULD YOU RATE THE DAY?

☆ ☆ ☆ ☆ ☆

3 THINGS I WISH FOR TOMORROW:

O _____

O _____

O _____

147

DOODLES AND DREAMS

date:

topic:

Dreams and Vision Goals

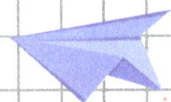

PRINCIPLE # 38
ALWAYS BE TEACHABLE

If you want to keep moving forward in life, you must be growing personally. In order to grow personally, you must be teachable.

If you ever get to a place when you think that you know it all, you stop growing.

Consider the following: We are all lifelong learners. Stay teachable.

We are all lifelong learners.
Why do you think that being teachable is so important?

"What I believe is that all clear-minded people should remain two things throughout their lifetimes: Curious and Teachable."
-Roger Ebert

Pamela Perez, The Education Therapist™

This page is intentionally blank for additional vision items, journaling, or so that the principle on the reverse side can be laminated and used as a poster.

5 MINUTE JOURNALING

Reflections

TOP 3 GOOD THINGS TODAY:

O _____

O _____

O _____

WHAT EMOTIONS HAVE YOU FELT TODAY?

HOW WOULD YOU RATE THE DAY?

☆ ☆ ☆ ☆ ☆

WHAT INSPIRED YOU THE MOST TODAY?

3 THINGS I WISH FOR TOMORROW:

O _____

O _____

O _____

DOODLES AND DREAMS

date:

topic:

Dreams and Vision Goals

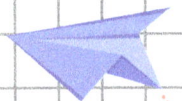

PRINCIPLE # 39
FACE YOUR FEARS

If you have big dreams for your life, you will encounter many challenges along the journey. Fears are there only to challenge you to grow, if it doesn't challenge you, it will not change you!

The word FEAR stands for False Evidence Appearing Real. It only exists in your mind and you can overcome it but first you must face it.

Most of the fear that we experience is learned. Some therapeutic models teach that you must expose yourself to it in order to overcome it. Identify one of your greatest fears. What ways can you expose yourself to it in order to conquer it?

"I learned that courage was not the absence of fear, but the triumph over it. The brave man is not he who does not feel afraid, but he who conquers that fear.
-Nelson Mandela

Pamela Perez, The Education Therapist™

This page is intentionally blank for additional vision items, journaling, or so that the principle on the reverse side can be laminated and used as a poster.

5 MINUTE JOURNALING

_____

_____

_____

_____

_____

_____

_____

_____

_____

_____

_____

Reflections

TOP 3 GOOD THINGS TODAY:

O _____

O _____

O _____

WHAT EMOTIONS HAVE YOU FELT TODAY?

WHAT INSPIRED YOU THE MOST TODAY?

3 THINGS I WISH FOR TOMORROW:

O _____

O _____

O _____

HOW WOULD YOU RATE THE DAY?

☆ ☆ ☆ ☆ ☆

155

DOODLES AND DREAMS

date:

topic:

Dreams and Vision Goals

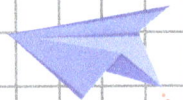

PRINCIPLE # 40
LET YOUR LIGHT SHINE!

There is a fire power within each one of us. Our responsibility is to learn how to ignite the fire and allow our light to shine in the world. What specific purpose do you believe that you were born for and how can you let that light shine for others to see?

"Our deepest fear is not that we are inadequate. Our deepest fear is that we are powerful beyond measure. It is our light, not our darkness, that most frightens us. Your playing small does not serve the world. There is nothing enlightened about shrinking so that other people won't feel insecure around you. We are all meant to shine as children do. It's not just in some of us; it is in everyone. And as we let our own lights shine, we unconsciously give other people permission to do the same. As we are liberated from our own fear, our presence automatically liberates others."
-Nelson Mandela

Pamela Perez, The Education Therapist™

This page is intentionally blank for additional vision items, journaling, or so that the principle on the reverse side can be laminated and used as a poster.

5 MINUTE JOURNALING

Reflections

TOP 3 GOOD THINGS TODAY:

O _____

O _____

O _____

WHAT EMOTIONS HAVE YOU FELT TODAY?

HOW WOULD YOU RATE THE DAY?

☆ ☆ ☆ ☆ ☆

WHAT INSPIRED YOU THE MOST TODAY?

3 THINGS I WISH FOR TOMORROW:

O _____

O _____

O _____

DOODLES AND DREAMS

date:

topic:

Dreams and vision Goals

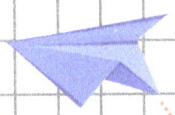

Pamela Perez, the founder of WAY Education Services, is an educator, psychologist, writer, and entrepreneur. Her educational background includes a specialist degree in Educational Leadership and a master's degree in Psychology. WAY Education Services was inspired in part by her last 15 years of experience as a high school teacher in the Florida Public Education System.

Ms. Perez now brings her professional expertise and the many highly valuable experiences in educational leadership to a wider classroom. In her books, published articles, and interviews, Ms. Perez offers up wisdom gleaned through hands-on observation in the educational system as well as her own journey of personal growth. She hopes to empower students, teachers, and administrators alike to tell their stories of hardship and triumph in and out of the classroom.

Ms. Perez says, "I can personally see the need now more than ever for students to be equipped with the knowledge to live a more meaningful life. Life is about order and principle, which is rarely ever taught in our schools. This type of education will be lifelong and well worth the study. Let's call it Life 101."

Her passion is to educate students on life principles that will continue to educate long after their formal education is completed. As a classroom teacher, she discovered that what we learn about ourselves is the greatest lesson of all.

She encourages students, teachers, and parents with these truths, "Mainstream education only teaches a small sector of what is important in life. There is so much more to a student than what is currently addressed in the classroom."

"We learn by instruction, but more importantly, we learn by what we discuss, what we personally experience, and teach others."

Ms. Perez has discovered and founded WAY Education Services on the belief that it is vital to educate the entire student, not just the intellectual part of the student. Every student has gifts, talents, and abilities. Those gifts and talents should be nurtured and developed so that the student is left with a life lived on purpose—a life that has meaning and value. This is a life worth living!

Pamela Perez, The Education Therapist™

161

SECOND EDITION

Available in eBook and paperback at your favorite online bookstore, or

To Purchase Additional Copies:

www.wayeducationservices.com